SCARY ADVENTURES AROUND THE WORLD

DO YOU DARE VISIT DEATH VALLEY?

BY MEGAN QUICK

Enslow PUBLISHING

Please visit our website, www.enslow.com. For a free color catalog of all our high-quality books, call toll free 1-800-398-2504 or fax 1-877-980-4454.

Library of Congress Cataloging-in-Publication Data
Names: Quick, Megan, author.
Title: Do you dare visit Death Valley? / Megan Quick.
Description: Buffalo, New York : Enslow Publishing, 2024. | Series: Scary adventures around the world | Includes bibliographical references and index.
Identifiers: LCCN 2023000448 | ISBN 9781978535916 (library binding) | ISBN 9781978535909 (paperback) | ISBN 9781978535923 (ebook)
Subjects: LCSH: Death Valley (Calif. and Nev.)–Juvenile literature.
Classification: LCC F868.D2 Q535 2024 | DDC 979.4/87–dc23/eng/20230201
LC record available at https://lccn.loc.gov/2023000448

Published in 2024 by
Enslow Publishing
2544 Clinton Street
Buffalo, NY 14224

Copyright © 2024 Enslow Publishing

Portions of this work were originally authored by Grace Vail and published as *Death Valley*. All new material in this edition was authored by Megan Quick.

Designer: Tanya Dellaccio Keeney
Editor: Megan Quick

Photo credits: Series background Le Chernina/Shutterstock.com; cover, p. 1 Bill Perry/Shutterstock.com; p. 4 Oscity/Shutterstock.com; p. 5 sigurcamp/Shutterstock.com; p. 7 (top) Rainer Lesniewski/Shutterstock.com; p. 7 (bottom) https://upload.wikimedia.org/wikipedia/commons/9/9a/Death_Valley_Mesquite_Flats_Sand_Dunes_2013.jpg; p. 9 Everett Collection/Shutterstock.com; p. 11 George Aldridge/Shutterstock.com; p. 13 (top) Dominic Gentilcore PhD/Shutterstock.com; p. 13 (bottom) https://upload.wikimedia.org/wikipedia/commons/3/37/Cyprinodon_diabolis%2C_males.jpg; p. 15 Jeffrey T. Kreulen/Shutterstock.com; p. 17 kavram/Shutterstock.com; p. 19 (top) Zack Frank/Shutterstock.com; p. 19 (bottom) Gchapel/Shutterstok.com; p. 20 fotomak/Shutterstock.com; p. 21 Isogood_patrick/Shutterstock.com.

Printed in the United States of America

CPSIA compliance information: Batch #CSENS24: For further information contact Enslow Publishing at 1-800-398-2504.

Find us on

CONTENTS

Words in the glossary appear in **bold** type the first time they are used in the text.

A HOT SPOT

Death Valley might not sound like somewhere you would want to visit. But if you like **extreme** heat, it could be the place for you! In fact, the air in Death Valley holds the record as the hottest in the world.

You might wonder if there's any life in Death Valley. The answer is yes! Plants, animals, and even some brave people live there. Let's learn more about this amazing area and see if it's as scary as it sounds.

BADWATER BASIN
282 FEET / 855 METERS
BELOW SEA LEVEL

FIND THE FACTS

DEATH VALLEY IS HOT, DRY... AND LOW! AN AREA CALLED BADWATER BASIN IS THE LOWEST POINT IN NORTH AMERICA. IT IS 282 FEET (86 M) BELOW SEA LEVEL.

In 1913, the air in Furnace Creek reached a world record of 134°F (57°C) that still stands.

WHERE IS DEATH VALLEY?

Death Valley is in the southwest United States. It lies mainly in southeast California, with a small section in Nevada. Death Valley is about 140 miles (225 km) long and 5 to 15 miles (8 to 24 km) wide. It is part of the Mojave (moh-HAH-vee) Desert.

Death Valley sits between several mountain ranges. To the west are the Panamint Mountains, and to the east are the Black, the Grapevine, and the spooky-sounding Funeral Mountains.

FIND THE FACTS

DEATH VALLEY WAS NAMED A NATIONAL PARK IN 1994. THIS MEANS THAT DEATH VALLEY IS A SPECIAL AREA WHOSE PLANTS, ANIMALS, AND RESOURCES MUST BE KEPT SAFE.

NEVADA

CALIFORNIA

DEATH VALLEY

This map shows the areas of Death Valley that lie in California and Nevada.

THE STORY BEHIND THE NAME

Death Valley got its name in the winter of 1849–50. At that time, **pioneers** were traveling west to California, hoping to find gold. One group of travelers decided to take a shortcut through the valley instead of taking the longer, safer route. It turned out to be a bad idea.

The group became stuck in the valley and wandered for weeks, tired and hungry. They finally made it out over the mountains. As they left, someone said, "Goodbye, Death Valley."

FIND THE FACTS

DEATH VALLEY'S NAME CAME FROM THE PIONEERS' BELIEF THAT THEY WERE ALL GOING TO DIE IN THE VALLEY. IN FACT, ONLY ONE PERSON FROM THEIR GROUP DID NOT MAKE IT OUT ALIVE.

In the mid-1800s, pioneers believed they could become rich by panning for gold, as seen here.

A HOME IN THE DESERT

A surprising number of animals live in Death Valley. They have **adapted** to survive in the hot, dry desert. Kangaroo rats do not need to drink any water—they get all they need from eating seeds. Roadrunners have a high body **temperature** and are not bothered by the heat. Animals like bighorn sheep move up higher in the mountains to cool off.

Death Valley gets busy at night! Many animals, like coyotes and jackrabbits, are nocturnal. This means they sleep during the heat of the day and hunt at night.

Wild **burros** were brought to Death Valley in the 1800s by miners and travelers. They can now be found all over the valley.

FIND THE FACTS

IF YOU DECIDE TO VISIT DEATH VALLEY, WATCH YOUR STEP! LIZARDS, RATTLESNAKES, AND SCORPIONS ARE COMMON IN THE DESERT.

LITTLE FISH IN BIG DANGER

There is not much water in Death Valley, so fish are hard to find. You'll need to go to Devils Hole, a pool in a deep **cavern** in Nevada. The Devils Hole pupfish lives there in the pool's warm waters.

Death Valley is the only place in the world where these pupfish are found. There are not many of them. There were 263 counted in 2022. That's more than there were 10 years ago! But they are still in danger. Any small change to their tiny **habitat** could be very harmful.

This small opening in the ground leads to the pool where Devils Hole pupfish live.

FIND THE FACTS

DEVILS HOLE PUPFISH ARE ONLY ABOUT 1 INCH (2.5 CM) LONG. THEY WERE NAMED FOR THE WAY THEY PLAYFULLY MOVE AROUND LIKE PUPPIES!

LIFE BLOOMS IN DEATH VALLEY

Believe it or not, Death Valley has lots of plant life! The valley's lowest parts only get about 2 inches (5 cm) of rain a year. There are not many plants there. But in higher areas, more rain means more plant life. In fact, Death Valley has more than 1,000 kinds of plants.

Like animals, plants have adapted to the hot, dry **climate**. About 50 types are only found in the special conditions of the valley. These plants often have roots that grow very deep or spread wide in search of water.

It does not rain often in Death Valley. But when it does, wildflowers pop up quickly!

FIND THE FACTS

THE CACTUS IS A DESERT PLANT. BUT THE FLOOR OF DEATH VALLEY IS SO HOT AND DRY THAT EVEN CACTI HAVE A HARD TIME SURVIVING! THE PLANTS ARE MAINLY FOUND IN THE HIGHER PARTS OF THE VALLEY.

SAND SONGS

Death Valley's sand **dunes** are one of the area's most famous features. In some places, mountains of sand rise up as much as 680 feet (207.3 m). And on a windy day, you might be able to hear the sand sing!

How can sand make noise? High winds can cause sand to slide down the steep dunes. It makes a low, booming sound. Some people say it sounds like an organ note! Scientists believe the sound comes from **energy** in the moving sand.

Many people imagine sand dunes when they think of Death Valley, but they actually only cover about 1 percent of the valley.

ONLY GHOSTS REMAIN

Would you like to visit a ghost town? Death Valley has quite a few! Starting in the mid-1800s, pioneers looking for riches traveled there to work in gold, silver, and copper **mines**. Towns grew quickly as more people came.

By the early 1900s, many of the mines were used up. There was no reason for anyone to stay in such a hot, dry climate. People **abandoned** the towns. In some areas, there's no sign that anyone ever lived there. In other places, homes, banks, and stores still stand empty.

FIND THE FACTS

DON'T EXPECT TO FIND ANY GHOSTS IN A GHOST TOWN! THE TERM IS USED FOR PLACES THAT USED TO BE BUSY AND CROWDED BUT NOW HAVE FEW OR NO PEOPLE LIVING THERE.

A shop stands in the ghost town of Rhyolite. At one point, the town had as many as 10,000 people, with churches, stores, saloons, and even an opera house.

DO YOU DARE?

Death Valley has extreme heat, rattlesnakes, and ghost towns. Each year, visitors who are not prepared with enough water and food have become sick or even died. At times, it can be a scary place! But it is also full of natural beauty as well as **unique** plant and animal life.

Do you dare visit Death Valley? You would not be alone! The area has more than a million visitors a year. If you come prepared, it could be a trip that you will never forget!

FIND THE FACTS

YOU MAY FEEL LIKE YOU ARE ON ANOTHER PLANET WHEN YOU VISIT DEATH VALLEY. IN FACT, SEVERAL SCENES FROM THE *STAR WARS* MOVIE SERIES WERE FILMED THERE.

Death Valley has some of the darkest night skies in the United States, which makes it a perfect spot for stargazing.

GLOSSARY

abandon: To leave empty or uncared for.

adapt: To change to suit conditions.

burro: A small donkey.

cavern: A large underground cave.

climate: The average weather conditions of a place over a period of time.

dune: A sand hill created by wind.

energy: Power used to do work.

extreme: Great or severe.

habitat: The natural place where an animal or plant lives.

mine: The pit or tunnel from which rocks and other matter are taken.

pioneer: One of the first American settlers to travel to and settle in the West.

resource: A usable supply of something.

temperature: How hot or cold something is.

unique: One of a kind.

FOR MORE INFORMATION

Books

Cosson, M. J. *Welcome to Death Valley National Park*. North Mankato, MN: Child's World, 2018.

The National Parks. New York, NY: DK Publishing, 2020.

Websites

National Park Service: Death Valley
www.nps.gov/deva/index.htm
Learn about the park's history, wildlife, people, and geography.

Visit California: Death Valley National Park
www.visitcalifornia.com/experience/know-you-go-death-valley-national-park/
Find out about more of the hot spots to visit on your trip to Death Valley.

INDEX